# On *Tok*

T0191313

"Sam Truitt has added a wonderful new innovative example of one of my favorite genres—travel poetry. By way of two "T squares" (Times and Tiananmen), on the way to Japan, he generously expands the notational into double accordion-fold expanses: one typed and sculptural, one handwritten, drawn notation condensing sound, thought, perception and time. The reader is invited into the poet's process alternating between quicksilver caught thought to poems lifted to the next level of line-break shape and form. The notebook page determines each "song's" length, much as Kerouac does with his *Mexico City Blues,* each part fitting in a pocket notebook. Here Truitt scores his poems across vertical lines, creating a palimpsest that references both the verticality of written Japanese language cross-hatched with English, as well as flown-through clouds of sound gathering in storm. In this travelogue of the present moment back in time to a formative locale, what's here now? In this delightful map of the mind moving we are given both deft improvisation and sculptural thought-song of all senses played 'toward the most beautiful / place on earth 52 years / coming home.'"

—**Lee Ann Brown**, author of *Philtre: Writing in the Dark 1989-2020*

"Inscription and transcription, the two fundamental modes of literary composition, echo each other in this work. The texts alternate—notebook hand written, poem typeset— calling their relationship into a dialogue. We stop seeing one as the inevitable outcome of the other. The process of writing interweaves the autographic hand and the allographic type, the individual expression and the linguistic system. Are the works 'the same' in each version—or does the process engage us with the impossibility of their being identical to each other? The intimacy of writing as note-taking feels palpably present. We intrude on those personal pages, even in facsimile. By contrast, the public-facing presentation of the typeset texts feels bold, exposed, declaratively blunt in its directness. Throughout, the texts themselves constantly reference lines and notations, divisions and demarcations, marking personal time and actual space across coordinates of language. Tracking, tracing, defining, delineating—all the many terms of writing activate this work and its notational transits."

—**Johanna Drucker**, author of *Diagrammatic Writing*


"Pop testimony, an epiphany going from language to a linguistic beyond of sullen images (too good to be entropy, though), conforming the edge of a (self) reflective anthroposphere. This staccato rumination shows culture to be something less (and more) than the usual accumulation-in-progress of technical & folkloric victories. *Tokyoatoto* is fine funk."

—**Omar Pérez**, author of *Cubanology*

Tok
yo
a
tot
o

# *Tokyoatoto*

## Sam Truitt

**Station Hill Press**

Published by Station Hill Press, the publishing project of the
Institute for Publishing Arts, Inc., 120 Station Hill Road,
Barrytown, NY 12507, New York, a not-for-profit, tax-exempt
organization [501(c)(3)].

Online catalogue: www.stationhill.org
e-mail: publishers@stationhill.org

Designed by the Catskill Poetic Action Network
Author photo: Alexandra Truitt

Library of Congress Cataloging-in-Publication Data

Names: Truitt, Sam, author.
Title: Tokyoatoto / Sam Truitt.
Description: Barrytown, NY : Station Hill Press, [2020]
Identifiers: LCCN 2020019301 | ISBN 9781581771985
(paperback)
Subjects: LCSH: Truitt, Sam---Travel--Japan--Tokyo--Poetry.
Classification: LCC PS3620.R85 T65 2020 | DDC 811/.6--dc23
LC record available at https://lccn.loc.gov/2020019301

Manufactured in the United States of America

**...嵐 哉**

**...*arashi kana***

**...storm o**

—Basho
fall 1680
35°41'10.0"N-
139°47'37.8"E

There's an ad,
almost square,
framed in chrome,
covered by plastic sheet,
beat to hell in the open,
on a corrugated wall,
of an open mouth,
of teeth & upper gums,
almost perfect & you can see
the darker pink tongue stilly
cleft at its axis as it is open,
lips
—

I sense lipstick or gloss
—

a bit of nose & nostrils above
the gate of the teeth

Begin to show in SHK
OPEN

THERE'S AN AD, ALMOST SQ., FRAMED ?? of
CRIMSON ?X COVERED BY ? [PLASTIC] SHEET
OF AN OPEN MOUTH, OF TEETH ? OR UPPER
GUMS, ?? MORE PERFECT ?? YOU CAN
SEE THE DARKER PINK TONGUE STILLY
CLEFT OF ITS AXIS AS THE MOUTH IS
OPEN, LIPS — I SWEAR LIPSTICK OR
GLOSS — A BIT OF NOSE AND NOSTRILS ABOVE
THE GANG OF THE TEETH

on the boulevard a cop car its
cherries & berries flashing I
see through a tight mesh grate
on a platform hook right down
a residential street,
& all the cars passing pausing
or parked tagged w/ dazzling
patches of sunlight reflected off
hoods & roofs,
& I am in one in my grate
window fingers in the mesh
holding on wondering why
keep going clawing by bus &
train & plane let alone hands
toward Tokyo by way of Peking
—
hoping I may cop the day pass
to walk the periphery of T Sq
as though ca. half a world
away some existential
exegetical geometry by which
to fit into a conspiracy of ads,
when what we really need are
minuses,
less,
sticking straight up through not
a wall as what spills through
them,
fingers

ON THE BLVD. A COP CAR ITS CARLAWETS PLAYING & BERRIES

I SEE THROUGH A TIGHT MESH GRATE ON
A PLATFORM HOME RIVING DOWN A RESIDENTIAL
STREET & AT THE CARS PASSING BY CARS
R BARKED
THROUGH WITH A DAZZLING PATCH OF
SUNLIGHT REFLECTED OFF THEIR HOODS &
ROOFS AND I AM NO ONE NO MAN
GRATE WINDOWS FRAMES FIGURES IN THE MESH
THRONG OR WONDERING WITH KEEP GOING

CLOSING BY BUS & THEN A PLANE WEST
ALONE HANDS TOWARD TOKYO RM WHY OF
PARKING — HONKING I MAN COP THE DAY PASS
TO WALK THE PERIPHERY OF TT SQ AS THROUGH
CD. HALF A WORDS AWAY SOME EXISTENTIAL
EX OF OPTICAL EGONEERING BUT WHERE TO FIT
INTO A CONSPIRACY OF ADS, WATER CLOSET
LOSS,
OF ANYWAY NEVER HERE MINUSES/STICKING
SPINNING UP THOUGH WAR A WALL AS
WORLD SPILLS NO. THROUGH THEM —

flesh

—

white flesh against steel mesh

—

or out the mouth of the security
snake put in place to strangle

—

what?

—

I have just passed through
shaken,
as even as I carry no
contraband or record or
exposure,
I swear,
I am at heart a criminal & so
watch my step & follow the rule
to not become a problem &
help people as much as I am
able to get through the wall or
maybe me too keep taking
away thought by thought
grooving to the terminal
countdown ethno-acoustico
atmospheros hum all below the
muzak what colleagues friends
& family form

FLESH... WRITE FLESH AGAINST STEEL
MESH — OR OUT THE MOST OF THE
SECURITY STAFF BUT IN ORDER TO
STRANGLE — WHAT? — I AM JUST
(PASSING) THROUGH SHAKEN, AS EVEN AS
I CARRY NO CONTRABAND OR
RECORD OR EXPOSURE, I SWEAR, I AM AT
HEART A CRIMINAL & SO WATCH MY

STEP AND FOLLOW, THE RULE TO NOT
BECOME A PROBLEM AND KEEP PEOPLE AS
I AM ABLE TO GET THROUGH THE
WALL A MEMBER ME TO KEEP TRACK OF
MYSELF THROUGH AN INSTANT GROWING IN
THE DRAMATIC ACOUSTICS OR AN ABOVE THE
(ATMOSPHERICS) & (FEAR) MUZAK
HUMS FLOWS
AS COLLEAGUES FRIENDS & FAMILY FROM

6

these knots these hills &
hillocks that are probably
mountains of sound shapes
that seem to correspond to
those through whom they
speak what speaks them w/ the
sun out the slated wall of glass
behind me at the bar low in the
sky across the tarmacs & the
fins & tails of planes the air like
the dirty martini the bartender
is pouring & it's sad to report
those of us alone are all
enscreened un-talking scrolling
or tapping swiping staring into
cell phones in a Borgesian leap
in some escape
—

just like I'm on this page
—

or rescue mission
—

if there were anything to leave
or retrieve
—

our collective ennui
—

or eyes like those of fishes in
the pits of oceans a lantern
—

or maybe there is a past &
future in this pass where these
two empty gates

THREE KNOTS THREE HILLS & HOLLOCKS
OF SOUND SHAPES THAT SEEMS TO
CORRESPOND TO THOSE (WITH) WHOM THEY
SPEAK? WHAT SPEAKS, THE SUN OUT THE
SLASHED WALL & CLEARS DESCEND IN AT
THE BAR LOW ON THE SKY? ACROSS THE
THOMAS AT THE FINS & TAILS OF PLANES
LIKE THE ADDI MARTIN THE BREAKWARE IS

POUNDING & ITS SAD TO REPORT THOSE
OF US ABOVE ARE FAR ON CALL PLANES
SCREAMING & MEANS of SIGNAL INTO
A SCREAM IN SOME BORGESIAN LAND OF
I AM ON THE BAR RESCUE MISSION - IT
THOSE WHOSE ATTEMPTS TO (ESCAPE) LABOR
AT RETRIEVE — OUR COLLECTIVE ENNUI —
ON SUCH LIKE MOSH of FISHES YOU — A
MANOR THERE IS THE PAST & THE FUTURE
IN THE GRASS WHERE THOSE TWO GATES

THIS FOR ENCLOSING PARTNERS

two storms

—

meet I stand perplexed signing
one

—

single file

—

in an inclined box w/ laminated
white pasteboard walls on
which are images of NY
sponsored by HSBC,
as I recall a Scottish bank
founded in Hong Kong,
which China is in the process
of absorbing though it will
make it good & sick & maybe in
some part kill it as it has been if
the future there is toward
higher & higher threshold of
individuation & determination in
the privilege engine as I have
sometimes disbelieved as the
wave of zombie logosicians
may meet & cancel it,
as I think two waves may as in
T Square that again I hope I
may stand in by way of the
Artic that I see we will be flying
over late at night the dark on
Earth on its highest edge

STRAIT NOTES ~ I STAND SINGLE FILE REPLEATED SIGNAL OMC
IN AN INCLINED BOX WITH LAMINATED
WALK PASE STAND WALLS ON WALKA
AS IN A WINDOW OF NY SPONSORED BY HSBC.
THAT WAS AN SCOTISH BANK FUNDED IN
HONG KONG WHICH CITANK IN THE
PROCESS OF ABSORBING THOUGHT IT WILL
WATCH IT GOOD A SIGE & MAYBE IT
SOLD THE BRANT KUG AS IT HAS BEEN

IF THE FUTURE THERE IS TOWARD DISTANCE &
VIRTUAL DIMENSIONS & INDIVIDUATION AS
I HAVE SOMETIMES DOUBTED IS THE MASS
OF ZOMBIE MAN MAYBE CANCER IS AS
I THINK TWO WAVES MAN AS IN T
SQUARE WHICH AGAIN I HOPE I MAY
STAND IN BY WAY OF THE ARCTIC THAT I SEE
WE WILL BE FLYING OVER LATE AT NIGHT
THE DARK OR EARLY ON ITS HIGHWAYS FOUR

if it were a page
--
so high that maybe there will
be light on the other side,
a slice which I guess would be
Russian sun not New York
Harbor turning over
Sheepshead Bay to pass as a
plane flies straight up the
Hudson & I fantasize my house
& Vergil curled in a ball on our
bed,
& Gigi & Indi in their rooms
engaged on respective
devices,
though maybe Vergil is w/ Eva
now who's w/ Mu & Kim in her
studio
—

which all sounds nice though I
know she's across the river
taking Eva to a Friends'
Thanksgiving & we are now
frankly over Long Island
subdivision though there
doesn't

So that from another there will be
light on the other side a
slice which I guess would be
Russia not New York harbor & meanwhile
use Streisand Bay to pass as a
plane flies straight up the Hudson
& I fantasize my horse & Virgil
curled in a ball on our bed &
Eva & Indi in other rooms

Embarks on devices thank maybe
Virgil is with Eva now who is
with Moon & Kim in her studio—
which all sounds nice though I
know she's across the river thank
Eva to a friends' thanksgiving
& we are now franklin are Lamb
Island subdivision thank that doesn't

seem anything left to subdivide
by or take away as there's no
not a square anything not
unoccupied except where cars
go & decency,
so the Cleavers aren't on top of
each other,
which maybe they are it being
Saturday & they're in a love-in
w/ their neighbors like in *The
Ice Storm* by Rick Moody &
now our flight path's changed &
we're lipping the edge of the
Connecticut coast which is
actually where Moody situated
his storm though through no
fault of his own as his parents
brought him into the world
there
—

or

seem anyone taken ahem as
means not a square to take survival anyone nn
occupied except where cans go
& decision so the cleaners.
aren't on top of each other —
what manner them are if break
saturday & they'll on a love-in
what their neighbors like on

the ice storm rn rock money
& now are front page? charged
& what'd lupton the face of the
connecticut coast which is actually
where money sinatra his storm
did'not mingle no faust or his
own or his parents bu banach
him into the world that — or

almost

—

one Saturday afternoon their
voices or cries drowned by a
passing plane & he thought I
really should write & organize
to have this flight path
changed,
though there really isn't any
other now only north &
darkness & a cabin in the sky
as we pass Sanikiluaq on our
way across Baffin Bay toward
Coral Harbour west of Cape
Dorset

—

so still a bit of land & lakes &
vast inland seas below & not
sure we'll ever actually leave

—

if we are not already

—

or should have gone to
Moscow to cross the North
Pole

—

& indeed while not quite hitting
it off the starboard wing there is
a band of horizontal light

—

Madonna

—

ALMOST — OUR SABBATH AFTERNOON
MEAL VOYGE DR GROFF DANNER
OUT AM A PRESENT AIRPLANE
& AT THROUGH I RATHER SHOULD
HAVE ORGANIZE TO HAVE THIS FLIGHT PLAN
CHANGED THOUGH THERE ISN'T ANY
COFFEE NOW ONLY NIGHT & DARKNESS
& A CABIN IN THE SKY AS WE

PASS SANIKILUAQ ON OUR WAY ACROSS
BAFFIN BAY TOWARD CORAL HARBOUR WEST
OF CAPE DORSET — SO STILL LAND OF LAND
BELOW & NOT SURE WE'LL A BIT ACHEVING EVER
LATER — SHOULD HAVE GONE TO MOSCOW
TO CROSS THE NORTH POLE — & INDEED
WHILE NOT QUITE ATTACK IT OFF THE
STARBOARD WING THERE IS A
BAND OF HORIZONTAL LIGHT MARDON-
A

32000 feet -59 F outside going
566 mph w/ a 25 mph,
or no or slim or negligible,
headwind
—

which must mean we are high
on the page
—

bearing about 1100 miles east
of Yakutsk about 863 s/w
Hotan 3373 past it while Omsk
is a bit more west yet in
distance
—

2410
—

a bit in between & closing,
as most sleep though two
Chinese men hang drinking
whiskey in the flight-attendant
corridor talking standing softly
laughing & sipping,
& it's almost like sex to be so
intimate & human unique
extraordinary to be roaring over
the ice like Rock Hudson in *Ice
Station Zebra*

32,000 FEET   -59 F OUTSIDE. COLD
  OR NO. SCRIM
566 MPH WIND @ 25 MPH HEADWIND.
  NEGLIGIBLE
BARROW ABOUT 1100 MILES FAR

JAKUTSK ABOUT 863 S/W, KHOTAN
3373 FEET IS WHITE. OMSK IS
A BIT MORE WEAR WAY IN DISTANCE
2410  A BIT IN BETWEEN 2

CLOSING, AS MORE SLEEP TONIGHT
TWO CHINESE MEN HAVE DRUNKEN
WHISKEY IN THE FULL FLIGHT ATTEN-
DANT CORRIDOR, TALKING SOFTLY
LAUGHING & SIPPING & IT'S ALMOST
LIKE SEX TO BE SO INTIMATE &
HUMAN UNIQUE FAR AWAY TO
BE ROARING OVER THE ICE LIKE
ROCK HUDSON IN ICE STORM ZEBRA

about submarines in an
awkward spot w/ their Russian
counterparts
—

as we scoot over Siberian ice &
crags & rock & out the grey &
purple river-looped land in the
orange light band I guess must
now be south as north
becomes it,
who knows?
—

it's Siberian late fall
—

I see a single light on what
appears might be a lake,
some cat in the shed Zen
butchering a reindeer in the
midafternoon which it appears
to be or flying past into
yesterday I've lost track of
time,
as though that were not
something
—

not unlike this airport where
through two gated transits I got
outside where it's dark &
nothing to do low 30's
manageable though T sq. is

ABANT SUBMARINES IN AN AWKWARD
SPOT W/ THEIR RUSSIAN COUNTERPARTS —
AS WE SCOUT OUR SUBTERRAN ICE & CREVS
OF ROCK A OUT & THE WAY A PURPLE RIVER
LOOKED LIKE IN THE ORANGE WATER BAD
~~OVER~~ I GUESS WHAT MUST NOW BE
SOUTH — WE SO IT'S SUBTERRAN ~~WINTER~~ CAN FALL
I SEE A SIMILAR LIGHT ON THE WALL
APPEARS MIGHT BE A LAKE — SOME
ARE OF THE SHEED WATCHING A RAMBLER

IN THE MID AFTERNOON WHICH IT
APPEARS TO BE OR FLYING AND INTO
EVENING I'VE LOST TRACK OF TIME AS
THROUGH THAT WHEN SOMEHOW ~~THE~~ —
~~FALMOUTHS & FACES~~ NOT IN LIKE THIS AIRPORT
~~WERE WHEN~~ THROUGH TWO GUARD
TRANSITS I GOT OUTSIDE WHERE IT'S
DARK & LOW 30'S MANAGEABLE ~~THROUGH~~
~~TO RUSH~~ A ~~KEEP~~ THROUGH T 50 'S

out

—

not enough time in these
meshes as though this were
someplace

—

so it is something

—

and now I've got a chance to
carve some arcs of devotion
through the airport as though I
were one which absent
signage & a change of tongue
& human form is just the same
as JFK,
though I am drinking a Tiger
beer & await a pizza w/ truffles

—

that's all I could understand

—

there's Christmas anthem
music on the hi-fi,
schmaltz choir sound

—

it's like I've died & arrived at a
terminal balcony eating area &
there's hardly anybody here as
all the smart set have lit into an
elsewhere locals hang
together,
though here I can watch
formula 1 racing or football

—

Strasbourg vs. Paris

—

I wish Merabi were here

—

out — not around here — so it is surprising & now I've got a chance to carve some arse at Oxotdon through the airport which absorb signage & a change of tongue & human form is just the same at JFK, though I am drinking a Tiger Beer & await a pizza of truffle — that's all I could understand — there's Canadian autumn music on the Hi-Fi — choir sound — real smaltz — it'll like I've died & come to a Terminal Bavary fastnel area & there's hardly anybody here as all the smart set have (shot) into an escalator where locals hang though here I can watch Formula 1 racing or football — Springbok or vs. Paris — I wish Marabi were here —

or turn my back or attention to
this vast domed enclosed
space of a few football pitches
lit by bands of light sets that
repetitively span its entirety the
working aspect of which aside
from this adjacent food balcony
is just 10 or so feet
—

though more the height of the
backboard,
so 13.5 in height actually
—

jive metal stands to dispense
tickets & take bags
—

so it's almost empty
—

what would Mao say?
    Decadent as a mogden.
    A car's gone off the track &
doing donuts that could fit
inside of here.
    It's still 0-0 in the match yet
there appears to have been a
dust up & a penalty kick
ensues
—

without issue,
kicked right into the crouching
goalie's chest.
    You can really taste the
truffle.
    Bricco where I am eating is
closed yet the nice server
person topped up my beer for
free.
    In this book I will thank her

an TRAIN of my BACK TO AND ATTENTION
TO THIS VAST DIMLY ENCLOSED SPACE of
A FEW FOOTBALL PITCHES LIT BY BANDS
of LIVING SKY THAT SPAN ITS ENTIRETY
THE WONDER ASPECT OF WHICH ASIDE FROM
THE ADJACENT FIRST CORRIDOR BALCONY
RIGHT JUST 10 or SO FEET SO IT'S
MOSTLY EMPTY — WHAT WOULD MAO
SAY? DECADENT AS A MCGOWEN.

A GAME'S GONE OFF THE PITCH & BOWLED
DONUTS WHILE COMING FOR SOMETHING OFF or THE MATCH
HAS THERE APPEARS OF WHAT TO HAVE BEEN A
OVER UP & A PHANTOM RIGHT ENSUES —
WITHOUT ISSUE, KICKED RIGHT INTO THE
CROWD GOALIE'S CHEST YOU CAN
REALLY HEAR THE TRAVELERS. THE BRICCO
WHERE I AM RIGHT IS CLOSED HER THE
NICE SALVER PERSON TOPPED UP MY
BEER FOR FREE. IN THIS BOOK I WILL

& try not to be plodding
recounting any getting my
syntax legs
—
yet see what this body or car
can do
—
which so far is nigh 1/2 the way
around the world to find not
much change or to retrieve or
rescue yet feeling great
—
fed & beerd & ready to
—
the lights are going out
—
they are properly closing
—
I must have just made it
—
my server has put on a jacket
—
the TV dark
—
and sprinted down a corridor
—
I will never see her again
—
it's just like Alice in her land of
wonder or one way to imagine
being dead
—
won't be seeing that again
—
transition via bewilderment &

A TRY NOT TO BE SO PEDANTIC RECOUNTANT
WHT AM I DOING MY ~~GRAMMAR~~ SIMPLY
VERBS SEEM WHAT THIS BOOK OR CAR
CAN DO WHICH SO FAR IS NEGH ½ THE
WAN AROUND THE WORLD TO FIND NOT
INVENT CHARACTER OR TO RETRIEVE OR
RESCUE HER FROM HER GREAT — FEED
& BRIGHTEN & REACH TO —— THE LIGHTS

~~DARK~~ ARE GOING OUT — MEN ARE
PARKING CLOSING — I MUST HAVE
JUST MADE UP — MY SERVICE HAS
PUT ON A JACKET — THE TV'S DARK —
& SPRINTED DOWN A CORRIDOR — I
WILL WATCH SEE HER AGAIN — IT'S
JUST EVER ALICE IN HER LAND
OF WONDER OR OUR WAY TO IMAGINE
BEING DEAD — WON'T BE SEEING THEM
AGAIN — TRANSITION VIA BEWILDERMENT &

then forgetting all
—

poof rinse repeat
—

& now I have been in this case
at the face of the terminal like a
cadre sleeping on a bench &
subsequently orange lobby
chair w/ a host of Chinese
others caught b/w flights
getting a little shut eye which is
very little as all the
jackhammering is saved for the
night,
w/ some teams distant & others
close at hand & the
aforementioned light
undimmed it's an active
sensorium let alone the near
impossibility of hitting meat
nerve bone equilibrium reckon I
ought go walk in the Chinese
night yet also thinking I should
save my energy for 6 am when
the systems

ignite though I will need cash

—

as my new plan is the express
bus into the Forbidden sector

—

& then more sleep less noise
ca. 4 & a white "A" reflected
onto the steel & glass
enclosure of an elevator in
front of me which I can read,
having moved down the
terminal face & a little
Caucasian girl sleeps in front of
me expertly w/ her two parents
behind me sleeping

—

& they've brought blankets so
one might identify them as a
family of adept airport sleepers,
& I guess if you add them up
I've slept about five hours & I'm
getting closer to abandonment

—

maybe some sun soon though
on my last outdoor jaunt note
it's freezing cold though just
along a series

~~STARE~~ GOING ~~BACK~~ UP THAT I WILL

WARD CASH — AT MY NEW PLAN

V3 THE EXPRESS BUS INTO THE

FORBIDDEN SECTOR — A NEW MORE

SLEEP LESS NOISE CAR. Y

STEP1 A THERE'S A WHITE "A" REFLECTED

ONTO THE GLASS ENCLOSURE OF AN ELEVATOR

IN FRONT OF ME HAVING MOVED DOWN THE

TERMINAL BEFORE & A LITTLE CAVEMAN

GIRL SLEEPS IN FRONT OF ME SLOPPILY

WITH HER TWO PARENT BEHIND ME SLEEP IN

— & THEM, WE BRING OUR BLANKETS SO ONE

MIGHT IDENTIFY THEM AS A FAMILY OF

ADEPT AIRPORT SLEEPERS & I GUESS

IF YOU ADD THEM UP I'VE SLEPT ABOUT

FIVE HOURS & I'M GETTING CLOSER TO

ABANDONMENT — MAYBE SOME SUN SOON THOUGH

ON MY WAY OUT DOOR WHERE NOW ITS

FREEZING TRAVEL JUST ALONG A SHORE
        COLD

of columns w/ red LED
language scrolling across them
like a Jenny Holzer story or
sculpture.
   All told it's not a bad airport
aside from all the grips around
& having to flash them your
passport & ticket
—
& in fact get swabbed for bomb
particles
—
and there's no newspapers &
google seems disabled as
though there were a war going
on & I'm on an extraction
mission,
or a recovery one or one that
makes me try to sleep on a
hard bench doing lots of mental
tricks to get there in splotches
always surprised a whole hour
has gone by,
& I'm soon hitting some kind of
decision point as to whether I
ought risk hopping a bus into
town on a Sunday

OF COLUMNS WITH RED LED LANTERNS SCATTERED ACROSS THEM LIKE A JERRY POLTZER WORK. AN TOWN IT'S NOT A BAD AIRPORT ASIDE FROM ALL THE CHECKS AROUND & HAVING TO FLASH YOUR PASSPORT & TICKET TO THEM — & THE FACT THERE'S NO NEWSPAPERS & GOVERN SCENE DISABLED AS THOUGH THERE WERE A WAR GOING ON AND I'm ON AN EXTRACTION

MISSION OR A RECOVERY ONE OR ONE THAT MAKES ME SLEEP ON A HARD BENCH THEN TO DOING LOTS OF MENTAL TRICKS TO CHAT TABLE IN SPLOTCHES ALWAYS SURPRISED A WHOLE HOUR HAS GONE BY & I'm SOON HITTING SOME KIND OF DECISION POINT AS TO WHETHER I OUGHT RISK HOPPING A BUS INTO TOWN OR A SUBWAY

morning risking missing my
flight so I can stand on T sq.
gesturing like a clown.
    Late last night I noticed
there's a hotel I could have
made walking just to say I did
& have a drink & I'm glad I
didn't,
saving my juice for Japan,
& seriously thinking of getting a
cup of coffee & giving up hitting
the square which I have
thought about since the
beginning as the Chinese
imprison torture murder
Tibetan friends & so why wave
any more attention to their
bastard way,
of which Confucius & Laotzu
would be completely disgusted,
just as are all the saints over
avarice & money when all we
need is a simple hut etc.
—

see

though I'm pleased to see the
people prosper if you can call
this that in puffy coats & don't
get the sense the cats w/
whom I slept the night have
been much touched
—

more grazed if not dazed &
raked
(
I don't appear through here to
be thanking her enough
)
by the Miracle
—

or maybe it's a big capitulation
—

or maybe the faint of one that
at some rascally moment will
spring around & collapse the
whole irrational model built on
infinite GDP growth & we can
go back to living in squats in
bands or just walk as I have
this airport as it comes to life w/
crews returning to status & I
just watched a series of
workers male & female
dressed the same
—

one set in light brown
—

they work the johns
—

& one

THOUGH I'M PLEASED TO SEE THE PEOPLE PROGRESS
IN THEIR PUFFY COATS & DON'T GET
THE SENSE THE CATS WITH WHOM I SLEPT
THAT NIGHT HAVE BEEN MUCH TOUCHED —
NONE AMAZED BY NOT RATED — BY THE
MIRACLE — OR MAYBE IT'S A BIG
CAPITULATION — OR MAYBE THE TRUST
OF OUR TEAM AT SOME REFLECTIVE MOMENT
WILL SPRING AROUND & COLLAPSE
THE WHOLE IRRATIONAL MODERN BUILT

AN INFINITE GOP GRAVITY & WE
CAN GO BACK TO LIVING IN ~~SMALL~~
HUTS IN ~~AND TRIBAL~~ BANDS ~~THERE~~
OR JUST WALK AS I HAVE THIS AFTERNOON
AS IT COMES TO LIFE WITH CARS
DEFERRING TO STRIDE & I JUST WATCHED
A SCORE OF WORKERS MALE & FEMALE
DRESSED THE SAME — ONE SHE IN LIGHT
BROWN — THEN WORE THE JEANS — & ONE

in black w/ the word "security"
written on their backs
—

they don't really make me feel
it
—

what are they guarding?
—

yet these teams must gather in
scrums behind the scenes in
shadow to emerge on the
stage in one swoop as the
shop doors are thrown open &
the arrival & departure boards
flash & fill & the lovely cup of
capitalistic coffee w/ milk I sip
soothing & love this world w/ all
human lights & patterns & the
one inhuman one in the form of
a new moon w/ its belly down
—

a hammock
—

over Earth to the sound of
wheel squeal upon the
departure apron
—

the sound of a beehive or
swarm
—

roads everywhere come here
to leave

"simplicity, clarity & emptiness"
Pico Iyer writes in his charming
memoir book of Japanese
observance
—
as I've put on my sunglasses &
turned my back on China,
even as I am in one of its
basement rooms sitting beside
a young Japanese student
from Chiba w/ terrific English &
immediate recognition as
though we had known each
other since time began or close
& even shy,
it's all good,
as the air vents around us
rattle & passengers begin to
gather & I am still light one
good nap which I will save for
the flight as I keep reading
about Honmura & James
Turrell project there
—
it's great.
    The Japanese way is more

"Simplicity, clarity and fullness" is Pico Iyer waives in his charming Japanese observation book — as I've put & turned my book on my sunglasses ... as I am in one of its basement rooms ... beside a young Japanese man from ... terrible ... & immediate ... as ... we had known each other ...

... on close of a final day — it's not good as the rare views around us rather & passengers begin to gather. And I am still light or good map which I will save for the flight as I ... James Turrell ... great. The Japanese ... is more minus.

    That & quiet.

    This & that.

    Ratatattat.

    "I" is extra.

    To get to Tokyo from Beijing you must fly around North Korea.

    It is forbidden.

    Gliding downward through clouds & then under & cotton & black mountains in gold light I found myself inexplicably sobbing & I am still sobbing now gliding downwards tears in & spilling from my eyes toward the most beautiful place on Earth 52 years coming home.

    Riding the train to Kuramae in a crowded car holding it together & almost calm

—

as even in the press the air's

MINUS. THAT & QUIET. THAT & THAT. RATA-
TATTAT. "I" IS EXTRA.

To GET TO TOKYO FROM BEIJING
YOU MUST FLY AROUND NORTH KOREA
It IS FORBIDDEN
CIRCLING DOWNWARD DRAWN CLOSER &
THEN UNDER & OVER & BY MOUNTAINS IN
CLOUD WHERE I FOUND MYSELF

INEXPLICABLY SOBBING & I AM STILL
SOBBING NOW GLIDING DOWNWARDS
TEARS IN & STINGING FROM MY EYES
TOWARD THE MOST BEAUTIFUL PLACE ON
EARTH 52 YEARS COMING HOME.

RIDING THE TRAIN TO KURAMA IN A CROWDED
CAR AGAINST EACH OTHER TOGETHER & KNOWING
CALM — AS FAR AS THE PRESS THE AIR's

deciduous,
fresh & cool & everyone is too
—
yet realize I left Iyer's
handsome red book tucked b/w
seats in the plane discovered
when I opened my travel box to
sort things out,
so that resource is gone &
aside from it being a solid book
& present from Misha I don't
mind as I'm not crazy about
any intercessions,
sagacious as it may have
proved,
or prefer my sideways blunder
fumble foray focused on no fact
I may fathom from what rends
as I sit now at a round white
table beside the Sumida River
on the other side of a wall
—
tropical palms in posts placed
against it
—
remembering Tokyo is warm
though oddly on the same

Fresh & cool & everyone is too — the
rhythms. I like Tyler's handsome
red book Tyler's and staring out the
window on some wine but outer space
I open my travel bag to sort things
out so that everything is gone & ask
Ken to keep a good book and a present
for Krista — I don't mind as I'm
not crazy about him. instead sessions

Suggestions as it may match predict or
prefer my (Blue-ish +) Siamese between
fumble furry focused on no fail I
may freedom from what wrongs as I sit
now at a window where table below
the Sumida River on the other side of
a wall with tropical palms in pots
perhaps another — remembering Tokyo
is warm though oddly on the same

latitudinal wave within some
monster degrees of Peking
though on the Pacific & that
current,
the Kuroshio gyre,
that licks this archipelago of
islands offshore Asia w/ which
it shares some kind, though
spare,
like a care bear of hum the
sum of which is now haggard
after so many trials & miles as
may be measured in time
—
let's face it
—
taken hard & maybe yet to
come.
      The discarded lighters
puddled outside the Beijing
airport departure apron doors,
many full & some quite
handsome w/ dragons & tigers
voluntarily discarded,
their fire
—
my phone left last night hung
from its charging cable fallen
from the curtained bed I'd slept
inside to the bunk below inside
the curtain

LATITUDE WITHOUT SOME (FEW) DEGREES
OF BEARING MARKED ON THE PACIFIC
& THAT CURRENT THAT LICKS
THIS ISLAND OFF SHORE OF ASIA
WITH WHICH IT SHARES SOME KIND
... SPARE ONCE A LAKE BEAR
OF WARM THE SUM OF WHICH IS NOW
HOVERING AFTER SO MANY ... ...

& MILES AS MANY MORE ...
IN TIME — LET'S FACE IT — HARD &
MAYBE YET TO COME. THE (PROVERB) OF
DISCARDED LIGHTNESS OUTSIDE THE ...
... MANY FULL &
SOME QUIET ... ...
... VOLUNTARILY DISCARDED
MY PHONE ... FELL FROM THE ...
... I'D ...
SLEPT INSIDE ... CORD
TO MY ... AND THE ...

a shipmate sleeps inside
—

just like Tokyo
—

& untethered unwilling to bug
my unknown Queequeg I lay
awake worried I'd lose it
—

that a thief slept beneath me
—

and now stand in my pajamas
@ 6:48 or thereabouts w/
coffee in a niche on the street
writing this & smoking &
mulling when & if I will
reconnect w/ it that is all I have
to sequence time to a scheme I
may play my  drum inside,
& remembering Amsterdam
when I did fall in w/ some
thieves,
damp day as salary folks drop
from apartment bldgs. into  the
street like phones I hear a crow
caw it's okay let the drunk kid
reach Z & reconstitute A that
grows out his chest's center or
solar plexus,
if there is such a place
—

a ganglia of nerves the way
electrical wiring is

in Tokyo rooms as though I
knew this odd improvisation,
as some cords slung from
ceilings are thick as umbilical
cords while other lines thin as
horsehair glow,
& you wonder when the next
earthquake hits will explode
into showers of gold sparks
souls come freighted in,
as I roll & smoke & drink coffee
& have jumped 1000 times up
& down avoiding a rope I hold
in each hand via handles & run
along the river & taking a
shower & dressed & my friend
whom I've tattooed w/ my
worries like a Yakuza sleeps
on & hope the A at the end of
his unconsciousness will soon
peak out as it's 10 now & I'm
anxious to reconnect w/ my
sister & her spouse no doubt
up & concerned I haven't been
in touch & bad assumed I was
up

.

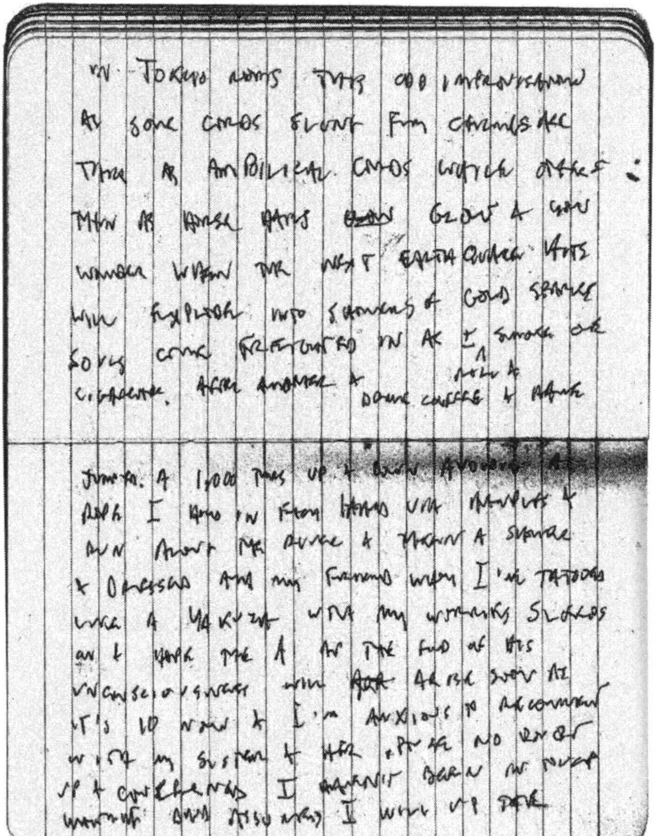

the night carousing passing
through the jaws of a 1000
dragons & mulling pulling the
curtain on him yet sense this a
greater criminal act than the
harm I keep on feeling sitting
cross legged at the apex of the
M,
or "mu" which means neither
one nor many up nor down &
not on & not out which a stalk
of bamboo sways.
        & then I went back &
messing w/ my chamber
かな
)
<u>kana</u>
)
saw his phone alight
—
checking the time?
—
& pounced & pow got my
coconut back & on & so I find
myself here again in a subway
car each of which feel like
being in a gumball machine at,
in counter-distinction to the
aboveground grey & grim
streets of Tokyo,
one festooned w/ bright faced
lettered ads w/ terrific comic
clown typographical details all
there to support these rings
that

hang down like empty gum
drops through which to see
them or stick your hands in
unintelligible bondage to
motion to very little rocking &
minus talk whisper into the
station to disembark & march
each moment a gate even if
you can't see them fall around
you in every direction &
dimension Tokyo full of gaijin
just like me or *Black Like Me*
the memoir of a white man who
dyed his skin dark & slipped
into the African American
stream he got shot out blood
poisoned to die not long after it
was written,
as I may
—

though I have no disguises
—

in this Golden Ku warren or
dinky bars catering to us
sucking our poison
—

aka money
—

out & I don't care if the roof is
on fire as it was 75 years back
when we fire-

HAVE DOWN LIKE ☆ FLIPPIN GUM
DROPS THROUGH WHICH Y SEE THEM IN
STICK YOUR HANDS REST (LOOK) (FOR WHAT)
BONDAGE TO MOTION TO SEE LITTLE ROCKET
A MINUS MINI WORKERS INTO THE JFK STATION
TO DIE FOREVER & ABSORB EACH MOMENT A
GHOST EVEN IF YOU CAN'T SEE THEM FALL
AROUND YOU IN EVERY DIRECTION & DIMENSION
TOKYO FULL OF GHOSTS JUST LIKE ME OR

BLANK LIKE ME THE MIRROR IN A WRITER
WHO DYED HIS SKIN & SLIPPED INTO THE
AFRICAN AMERICAN BLOOD SHOT & SHOT
AND IF IT POISONED TO DIE NOT LONG
AFTER IT WAS WRITTEN AS I AM
IN THIS GONDOW KU WARREN OR DONKEY
BARS CATERING TO US SUCKING OUR
POISON — AKA MONKEY OUR & I
DON'T CARE THE ROOF IS ON FIRE AS
IT WAS 75 YEARS BACK WHEN WE FIRE

2019
IGUH
/5

54

bombed this town to the
ground yet its bones are strong
& there is a sign over the bar
"Samurai Shot" & the
memories bring memories back
& the waves waves even if they
are of nausea,
as Sartre knew & groomed &
dated awhile as I am quietly
toasted drinking a last whiskey
after the sun fell as red or
bronze or whatever the true
hue of it will prove when we go
& become one,
though not as crazy all day
long having put in nine miles
hoofing Tokyo pavements &
much time w/ Alex & Jerry
enshrined & in ancillary
boneyards that in Japan are
highly & tastefully stylized
plinths of raw stone sometimes
adorned w/

BOMBED THIS TOWN TO THE GROUND YET
ITS ROOTS ARE STRONG & THERE IS A
SIGN OVER THE BAR "SAMURI SHOT" &
THE MEMORIES BRING BACK MEMORIES &
THE WAVES WAVES FLOW UP DOWN ALL
OF NASEAU IT IS SHRINE KNOWN &
GROOMED & DATED ANOTHER IS I AM
QUIETLY TOASTING DRINKING A WARM
WHISKEY AFTER THE SUN FELL AS
RED OR BRONZE OR WHATEVER THE TRUE

COLOR OF IT WHEN PRIDE WOULD
GO & BECOME IT WOULD NOT AS
WARM ALL DAY LONG BATING FOR
WINNING MINDS ROOFING THE PARKMENTS
& MUCH TIME WITH ALEX & JOREN
TOKYO
ENSHRINED & ANCILLARY BOULEVARDS
THAT IN JAPAN ARE HIGHLY & MASSIVE
STYLIZED PLINTHS OF RAW STONE
SOMETIMES ADORNED WITH

script though never enough to
mar nakedness the bone the
last sticks we play to on no
drum,
like the elderly man I saw on
the subway platform try in a
black suit to walk drunk in a
straight line & couldn't for the
life of him like I lisp
—

the difference b/w life & death
is sleep
—

or one good one,
the knit,
putting things together or
pulling them apart again,
yet it's still there
—

the dip
—

& the question
—

to put something there b/w us
we may climb down to or up as
I am to another of foreign letter
"un"
—

the page is the raft of
—

Earth a simple or complex
arrangement,
like "mu" which looks like a
house or mesh fence,
無
some roots or accents where
we touch a bridge,
across the Sumida in a general
rain wondering about

A BIT OF SCRIPT MAYBE NEARLY
KNOWING TO MAKE A NARROWNESS TO
THE BANK THE KEY STICKS WE PLAN
TO NO DRUM WHILE THE FREEDOM MAN
PLATFORM
(I SAW ON THE SUBWAY (DRUNK) TRYING
W # BLACK SUIT TO WALK KNOW A STRANGER
WORD & CONVEN'T FOR THE LACK OF
HIM LIKE I LISP — THE DIFFERENCE WORD
& SHARP IS SLANG — OR I COULD ONE — THE

KNOT — # PUTTING THINGS TOGETHER OR
PULLING APART — YES IT'S STILL THERE —
THE DIP — & THE QUESTION — TO PUT SOME-
THING THERE BETWEEN US WE MEAN CLIMB
DOWN OR UP & I AIM TO ANSWER OF
FOREIGN LETTER — US — EVEN A SIMPLER OR
WITH COMPLEX ARRANGEMENT — LIKE " MY"
WHICH LOOKS LIKE A HOUSE OR MESA
SOME ROOTS OR ACCENTS WHERE
WE TOUCH A BRIDGE ACROSS THE
SUMMER IN A RACE WONDERS ABOUT

the young man in the bunk
below mine who seems to be
embed all the time sleeping I
suppose he's always there
under blankets a dark head
against white sheets & maybe
he's sick or depressed or isn't
real or there,
though I am always quiet in our
room
—
there appear five of us
—
because of him like a mouse
not stirring the grass taking
extra time to click open the lock
or draw curtain or unclasp
valise that I may not break his
concentration & inwardly
hoping he will get enough rest
to get up,
& really would like him to,
so I could whistle & chirp &
sing & bounce around though
really for his

THE YOUNG MAN IN THE ROOM BELOW
MINE WHO SEEMS TO BE IN BED ALL
THE TIME (UNDER BLANKETS SUFFERS) I
SUPPOSE YET HE'S ALWAYS NEAR

A THE DOOR READ ALWANGL THE WANDE SQUATS
X MAYBE HE'S SICK OR PARALYZED
OR ISN'T ALIVE OR MAYBE THINK I AM
ALWAYS QUIET IN MY ROOM — THERE
APPEAR FIVE OR US — BECAUSE OF HIM

LIKE A MOUSE NOT SCARED THE
CLOSES THERE EXTRA TIME TO CLICK
OPEN THE LOCK OR DRAW CURTAIN
OR OPEN VALISE THAT I AM BREAK
ITS CONCENTRATION A INWARDLY
HOPING HE WILL HAVE ENOUGH REST TO
WAKE UP & REALIZE HOW HARD I LIKE HIM
NOT TO BE THERE SO I COULD
WHISTLE & STEP CHIRP & SING X
BOUNCE AROUND THROUGH RANDOM FOR HIS

own good find a

—

or even his

—

world to explore

—

is "mu."
    Tokyo natives seem to
really connect w/ umbrellas as
even if it's just grey more than
just keep an umbrella around
open it

—

yet there's no rain

—

& folded up its surface is
sword-like so must touch some
my semi-primordial samurai
association?
    Like sitting in some random
downtown lunch spot at the bar
watching how she carries two
cups of coffee in saucers & a
glass of ice in one hand w/ her
pinkie & plates of food in the
other shot across the
restaurant balancing the load
barking these salary men
around,
who understandably are a little
in love w/ her

OWN GOOD TO FIND A — A FATAL HIS —
WORLD TO EXPLORE — IS "ME"

TOKYO NATIVES SEEM TO REALLY CONNECT
W/ UMBRELLA AS FEW UP ITS TO STAY
WARM & SPIFFFD RATHER THAN THE WE
JUST KEEP AN UMBRELLA AROUND OTHER
IT — YOUR ITS NOT RAIN — & FOLD IT
UP THEREFORE IST A BIT LIKE A
SWORD SO MUCH TOUCH SOME PRIMORDIAL

SAMURAI ASSOCIATIONS. LIKE SITTING AT
SOME RANDOM DOWNTOWN LUNCH SPOT AT
THE BAR WATCHING HOW SHE CARRIES TWO
CUPS OF TO CORNER, & A GLASS OF ICE
IN ONE
                        ON
                    SAUCERS
    HAND WITH HER PINKIE (BALANCING THE
(AND) TROTED ACROSS THE RESTAURANT &
SETTLED BESIDE THE TABLE STREAM WHERE
AROUND BARKING WHO UNDERSTANDABLY
WAS A LITTLE IN LOVE WITH HER

CORRECTLY
NEEDLE IN
FULL & FLEW

<u>there</u>

Tokyo Tower shoots
out the roof of Zōjō-ji
why are you standing

& so having gone from god
knows where to god knows
where where we are in a
parking garage waiting out the
end of time that comes
wrapped in cellophane
—
not,
yet it's nice to make believe it
does enough that we may
package it in words that come
to squat in a parking garage &
feel the wave of what is to
come wash over one in the
distance of trash being taken
out
—
which is as much as in & why
are we still hung up in
Descartes when language is
itself one that breaks open the
husk of what is
—
as the old & new begin again
—
Tokyo

X SO WE HAVE COME FROM
GOD KNOWS WHERE & GOD
KNOWS WHERE WHERE WE
ARE IN A DISTANT WARREN
WAITING OUT THE END OF THE
TALE COMES WRAPPED IN
CELLOPHANE — NOT THE IT'S
EVER TO MAKE BEFORE
IT DOES ENOUGH THAT WE
CAN PACKAGE IT IN WORDS

THE LONG TO SEE SOOTHE ON A BARREN WHEEL
& FEEL THE WHAT THE WAY WHAT'S IS TO END WHICH
AFTER ONE IN THE DISTANCE OF THE THESE
BUT THEY ONE WHERE IS AS MUCH AS
IN X WAR NEAR THE SINK WHAT UP ON DESCARTES
ON MY CONTRANE IS PRESENT OF ONCE
THAT BREAKS OPEN THE HOUSE OF WHAT IS
AS THE OLD & THE NEW BORN AGAIN
— TOKYO

TOWER
THE TOKYO SHORE ONE/OUT
THE RINK OF DAIMARU
SHRINE WITH ROSE AND SHADOW TREE

The music of the Tokyo subway
system w/ everybody alone
together in what binds them
which is words I almost wrote
but rules
—
I want to say Omar here yet it is
not so & yet one senses a web
each of us hold together & yet
against & yet around us like a
net of civility not docility as there
are some faraway landscapes in
our mind & in our heart & our
bodies are dreaming all of them
uniting to listen to the
underground hum its magic
—
how that man leans on his arm
hanging to the strap wearing a
mask yet wearing a beige
raincoat like some London Fog
classic
—
which I think wild relative to the
black the millennians favor
—
breathing hard & I think holding
it all in
—
his guts

the gate in the Japanese sense
that potentiality,
not we hope sheep or being
penned or walking on the left
side of any way you can find to
get around yet never the gate
you must pass through to find
they repeat after me the poem
cannot be
—

you could say sex alone makes
it worth it yet even sex wears
thin & then you're stuck w/ a
habit of working & within a
structure,
as I see so many of my
Japanese kin are,
in absence mostly their even
being aware they're in the suck,
their auras barely don't fit inside
—

& so it goes back & forth until it
is gone

the 12 of us
—

we could be all be friends in the
car underground divided into
fours so there are three of us on
a seat the Japanese & me
feeling comfy though it is mostly
folks in their cells sunk into
program synchronized to the
system,
as though there were one & not
a collective hallucination at the
rock of which doors open &
people leave & people come in
like sentences,
& whatever is beyond them
which is us,
one breath as our pasts & the
people we have known connect,
including Harold Kalke whose
idea this that we have a car
we're on & people step on &
people step off,
like our families,
& I keep coming back that I feel
so

at home because of my
projection on my own past,
& happy to be alone to try to
catch up w/ it
—
marks,
like a shadow cast back where
there's no light behind my form
to catch
—
between which a life is
sandwiched,
a woman nodding off beside me
—
yet some vibration close to the
bone or what we leave as well
as have & teeth ghosts together
shooting underground in our
tunnels lips not moving in one
only odd vibration again of a
wire that passes through us
because of the rules,
& this symmetry of space b/w
people like a work of art
—
which Japanese culture may be
—
absent any contemporary one
(
according to Alex
)
& I just got off & a man domo
arregato'ed me & very solid
manifestation of the grace of this
place by stepping out behind me

on the platform handing me the
bag of things I have for my
nephew Duncan which would
have resulted in "stress" blowing
my mind bursting out of the
crowd in Midtown & so can't
smoke on the street which I want
to do to have this time to beside
myself on going into the Ritz
Carlton & the taut environment
calling not far away,
a tall building such as steel
girders made possible & flexible
enough to handle the Earth
quaking as I feel right now
explode into lights in all the trees
& some fountains that are lit
inside & some bushes also & the
people too passing along this
access path to the riches that
the bldg. may hold which I don't
account much yet meet Jerry in
15 minutes for a drink & no one
has hassled me

yet as I think perceive to the
symmetries of Japanese dress I
may appear a bum w/ heavy
biker boots & black pants & this
herringbone overcoat w/
unconventional collar
(
though remarkably like the
Japanese school uniform one
which I hadn't thought of in
choosing out clothes to bring
—

yet must have been something I
carried from here I am carrying
—

back
)
& zippers up my wrists which is
one risk yet nothing I will not
take to feel a cool breeze rise off
the bay & the cheerful chirp of
voices
—

Tokyo-a-toto

TOKYO-A
-TOTO

& this morning walking on a
fresh sheet of sun having
popped from a hole in the
ground called Roppongi Station
after a night of heavy drinking I
heard a crow call & as though I
hadn't gotten the message one
flew over my shoulders & I felt
nigh nip my neck & heard for the
second time in my walk across it
—

the first sitting on an outcrop on
the outskirts of Joshua
—

the rowing of wings
—

& they're still rowing the
incredible stillness in the local
place at a corner around the
kitchen two men work together
making meals you buy via a
vending machine & nobody talks
as the men do this choreograph
& I am thinking how I read
someplace that Japan is full of
advanced incarnations I feel now
watching these two cats dance
together a complete surrender to
each other

& to us these bowls & plates of
great food & drink & it's
performance art at its apogee as
it also feeds us physically & feel
the people when you can slow
them down enough caw like the
<u>Karasu</u>
—

except the sound of this slurping
& the racket of the kitchen where
what is made meets what is
making in what is said between
us as we talk via our handhelds
w/ each other
—

this one cat who seems to me
bouncer-up-mountains-around &
a big jazz afficionado & it went
on like this,
scrolls of steam rising from the
different pots

Cities are made for walking
endlessly the pavement rising in
different scales including height
as it comes up to meet you in
Kuramae,
which is one end of the rainbow,
made of different pockets the
one in which I'm in being the
river & a bridge which is all you
need to run a civil rhythm from a
rhyme such as we constitute
when we listen & are when we
are in it listening to it flow not so
gently as her big shoulders lift
Tokyo on its banks
—

the Sumida
—

among other rivers
—

& good access to bay & open
sea at her mouth made Edo the
supernatural capitol some
emperor sits inside in the body
of whose light beam we are
floating on endlessly rambling

CROSS all while for undefined Endless on
the pavement rising up in different
scales (to meet you) undefined
happen as it comes up to meet you
in knowledge which is made of
different pockets and in which
I'm in between a river & a
boulder where is the you need to

RUN A CIVIL-RHYTHM IZATION
Rhythm & Rhythm just as we constantly
when we are listening ... & ... when
we are ... to listening flow into that
so closely as the surface like a river
on its banks — and under rivers — the
sunday — a good access to all
that made from the supernatural
capital some explored just inside all
the body of which ... means we are
flowing on endlessly rambling

standing in a checkered plaza
on taupe & cream-colored tile
outside Meguro Station under
some brighter lights w/ others
around & road & traffic right in its
center,
so that Chidananda can't miss
me,
I wait to go to the house of
Yogmata & have been 20
minutes spinning around
periodically & in a way like much
of Tokyo it's a comfort to have a
layer of decision removed from
my person as for another 10
minutes respecting the half-hour
rule now there is nothing to do &
that's true,
blank stares

STANDING IN A CIGARETTE'S PUFFING AS
TOP OF A CREAM COLORED TRUCK A OUR
RAILWAY STATION UNDER SOME BRIGHT
LIGHTS WITH OTHERS AROUND &
ROAD & TRAFFIC RIGHT IN ITS GLARE
SO THAT CHIGASAKI CAN'T MISS
ME I WAIT TO GO TO THE HOUSE
OF YOGIWARA & HAVE SPENT 20 MINUTES
SPINNING GOING PERIODICALLY & IN

A WET LUNCH MUGGY OF TOKYO IT'S
A COMFORT TO HAVE A LAYER OF
DRY DRIZZLING REMOVED FROM MY PERSON
& FOR ANOTHER 10 MINUTES THERE IS
NOTHING TO DO &                    RESEARCH THE
THAT'S THEIR BLANK          HALF - HOUR WHEN
SIMPLE           1                | WON

                    ARIGATO
GOZI MASTA                   GOZIIMASU

the galling rains of Tokyo

—

everyone armed w/ swords

—

trying to find ways to hide from it

—

from them

—

the rains blowing off the Pacific
downing the town in rain
dropping from eaves & awnings
& the translucent umbrellas of
young women in white blouses &
black mini-skirts w/ thigh-high
stockings

NINJA Movie Recommend

Kuramae
↓ (Asakusa Line)                    ＡＫＩＡ

Asakusabashi
↓ (Soba Line)

Akihabara

THE SKYLINE RAIN OF TOKYO —
EVERYONE ARMED WITH SWORDS — TRYING
TO FIND WAYS TO HACK FROM 25 —
FROM RAIN — THE RAIN'S BLOWING OFF
THE PACIFIC BLOWING THE TOWN IN RAIN
DROPPING FROM FACES & DIE AMONGST
THE ... IMPOSSIBLE ... WITH
OF A YOUNG WOMEN IN BLACK BLOUSES
& MINI SKIRTS WITH BROWN STARS
BLACK          JAPAN — HER A STOCKINGS

their hair in two pigtails w/ red &
white ribbons
—
the colors of Japan
—
dancing a jig & not pressing
leaflets gently into the sullen
mass more than showing they
are there & bowing smiling up
her own sword too pointed at the
sky's cursed rain that keeps us
from coming up out the hole in
the ground toward where my
family was when I was small,
to step through the wind to
remember vaguely & fondly
Wakamasu-cho,
all you've got to do is turn
around to find where you came
from

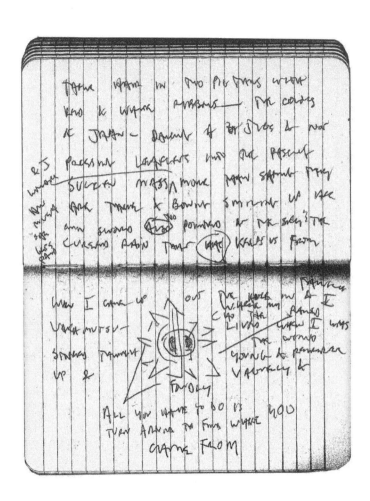

ALL YOU HAVE TO DO IS YOU
TURN AROUND TO FIND WHERE YOU
CAME FROM

FAMILY

hum
—

& the train coming into Shinjuku
does & the doors again open &
we're away again puzzling again
the path having already spaced
a transfer & interacting w/ Tokyo
sans handheld brings a bite &
actually focuses one to stay on
the path or at best awoke
—

even as even if I covered w/ the
crook of my arm a cough felt a
society cave in like I wasn't
there,
I felt myself so aware
—

& because of the blown circuit I
am back in Wakamatsu-cho not
grinding my teeth just happy to
hang w/ the people & write even
if literally everybody around me
is tapping &

swiping their cells,
pawing walls,
as though eager to climb
beyond
—
even as I am not having let its
juice lapse & I think the fact I
had had a charger masked the
fact its battery life was crap or
maybe I too,
trying to negotiate & photograph
for family this city,
am raging on its raft w/ abandon
slaloming through information
even if most of it's rotten & what
not
—
so your stalk sticks straight up
like a metal tip to better be
harvested or die for another
emperor,
even if it's an invisible one like
the devil or it might be the lord
like

James Clavell's <u>Shogun</u> when I
first learned the meaning of the
word "yes,"
& it's tragic to come to touch
some ichor to discover nothing
there,
unlike the Sumida which
glistening & full forces a course
in width as wide as two footfall
pitches of quietness though
traversed by the most common
sound in the human universe in
two directions
—

everything you don't leave is
breathing I am cosmopolitan
—

& everything else afterthought &
each crack a universe awaiting
us to open what we are always
in as now listening to traffic in a
din of lights w/ music coming
from somewhere w/ no place to
go more

Spoken Clarence's S140(gra) When I
first learned the meaning of the
word "yes" & it's theatre to come
to touch source before to discrete would
make & unlike the surreal which is
charming and full of imagination

Width as        familiar like a course
m what as two football friends of
quietness things thousands on the

most common sound in the human
universe comes away in the
dimensions following you don't think
43 Behavior or I am a cosmopolitan
& everything else is afterthought
& essey crack a universe anxious us
to clear (them) when we are always in as
now I hound to prattle in a box of
lights w/ music coming from somewhere
with nowhere to go more

95

the diamond at the end of the
palm of the known or that can't
be or dreamt or swept away by
thought that pulls to a stop & the
fare negotiated Charon pops out
the door to another way to the
river blocked off w/ trucks &
cones & a man in a security
uniform & hardhat standing at
attention beside one
—

just like me
—

his heart beating slower than the
jackhammer cracking a tidy hole
in the cement
—

not what is encased in
—

flesh
—

the river is
—

listening
—

as just now Earth moved & not
as Hemingway knew
—

side to side swaying like a tree
the building as folks pause &
resume,
as I check my left back pocket
dedicated to trash & right
tobacco pouch & filters & in my
left front one a money roll

& earphones & right one coins &
lighter & in the change/stash
pocket a secret nothing & so a
way out w/ everything I space
passport phone & this book
—
then
—

in left breast pocket of grey coat
w/ Tokyo collar a voice recorder
& right some lemon drops & to
cap it all the Georgian cap
Merab gave in the lip of which I
happen to keep a piece of jade
like Laotzu corresponding to the
third eye out which I see
nothing.
    Now,
I guess 150-odd years in, Japan
should close its borders again

MOCHI

ETA
DA KTE
MASU

GO CHI
SO USA
MA DE 3 H
TA

GO CHI
SO U V
DE SA, TA

There in green slanting cap
letters in the right upper corner
of the page that is a 12-story
office I guess building across the
Sumida I have a sign in sight
that reads <u>LION</u>
—
listen
—
& I am a merry one as I hold
between my hands the face of
the sun & were tawny & golden
as the Japanese are rising about
7 w/ it around us like a body of a
woman I feel her beside myself
rising too on her haunches
smiling like a Dakini who
whispers to me the names of
things I can only say back & will
never know,
as when I am w/ her I seem to
operate in the zone,
the end of which is near
—
what it means to be in the book
the pages of which are these
moments of pounce as a bird
—
<u>tori</u> 鳥
—
rises out of her w/ a fish in its
mouth to circle low on her to fly
up the middle channel

& under a bridge span that I
guess are her armpits,
& even the pigeons here seem
more civil self-aware & attentive
though they look the same & like
to comingle & integrate w/ the
shadows though there really
aren't many,
as now it's noon & anyway more
distinct its edges of darkness,
which actually is a seemingly
different form of light than in
northeastern north America
—

or sudden blackness,
like you experience in outer or
utter space
—

& now I'm crossing the bridge
working up w/ everything that I
can sitting about at its apex my
eyes out into the sun SE,
which I guess makes sense if
any direction does when my
center of gravity is bent, through
a bit more in balance,
or sound,
however asymmetrically of the
body blinded by the sun
—

& I guess it's the paucity of
softness that's different
—

the weather very sharp

here as I look into her rough
bank water & path luminosity
through her as a ship passes &
sends wakes through us going
every which way as I think the
Sumida is tidal I realize along w/
all the other things I don't know
about her,
along the shores of whom there
isn't much color,
except advertising
(
Mallarmé
)
I mean why doesn't somebody
paint their house fuchsia or
lemon yellow,
the color of the sun,
or cat eyes over the door I am
writing to find if there was a
mission & any forms of
manumission we may own or
owe the stones set into its walls
w/ psychodelic precision

HERE AS I LOOK INTO THE RIGHT HAND WIPER
AND PAINT LUMINOSITY TRAVELING LIKE AS
A SHIP PASSES A STARS WHICH THOUGH
IT GOING FAR WHICH WHEN AS I
THINK THE SUMMER IS THEN I REALIZE
AND ALL THE OTHER THINGS I DON'T
KNOW ABOUT HER EVEN WHICH WAY ABOUT
THE RANGE OF WHAT THERE ISN'T MUCH
COME FURTHER ADVERTISING I WHEN

WHEN OTHERS SOMEBODY PAINT THEIR
HOUSE FUSIA OR WINDOW WINDOW OR
CAR RINGS OVER THE DOOR I AM WITHOUT
TO FIND IF THESE WAS A MISSION
OR ANY FORMS OF MANUMISSION WE OUR
OWN OR OUR THE STONES SENT INTO THE WAYS
WHICH WITH HALLUCINOGENIC PRECISION

& remember the art here is
mutual understanding &
contemplation as a basis for
being born,
though as noted I could never
clock to it or I don't want to live
in a country the laws of which I
can't breathe,
even w/ a fist of light as I dream
of Tokyo & see how in Sumida
City or thereabouts
—
the page
—
on this long unwinding trip or the
river to the garden where when
you're standing you're red &
walking green again cross inland
—
& couldn't hack it
—
& claw my way back to her &
quietness & breathe awhile &
then press on to the garden
—
which I realize now having
repeated,
which I am actually living,
I've endowed w/ a lot of
credence,
though as I found in Wakamasu-
cho not worth much believing

or maybe skip the garden that is
very ancient & stay here on the
sun path,
but trudge on,
& you really have to wonder if
trying to make the garden is
worth the trip,
& better to get a contemplative
jag & relax into her body
everyone has a cell in
—

could there be a garden worth
leaving the river for?
—

as a European broad on a bike
sidling up knocks my tail that
caused my rhythm

to jerk & I'm walking through the
city w/ a bag of trash in my
armpit,
as the light is dying as suddenly
as my GPS says I've walked in a
wrong direction for 13 minutes,
as I must have been right up on
its arse a moment ago & failed
to connect
—

so I'm tired & maybe I will make
the garden at dusk,
or I will never make it or out
standing under a streetlight in an
alley now,
& as I wrote it turns out like I
was already there & now I'm
clawing my way back
—

yet the garden of the neverlife
closes at dusk & I can't keep

slogging through these bleak
homogenous streets & must fall
back as nothing is worth this
much effort
—
the wise twisted green adorned
flows of a Japanese cedar just
out of reach,
boughs of hands the eyes
complete,
which I watch in an alley that are
the living views of Tokyo
—
not the streets that are its asses
really
—
or feet or mind or some other
ugly part
—
not that the ass is,
winking at me,
as I have been up it
—
these backwater walk/bike ways
where there are flowers &
shrines set out & the sun on the
other side of some buildings an
old-fashioned antenna sticks out
—
maybe an old-school ham
operator remembering the war

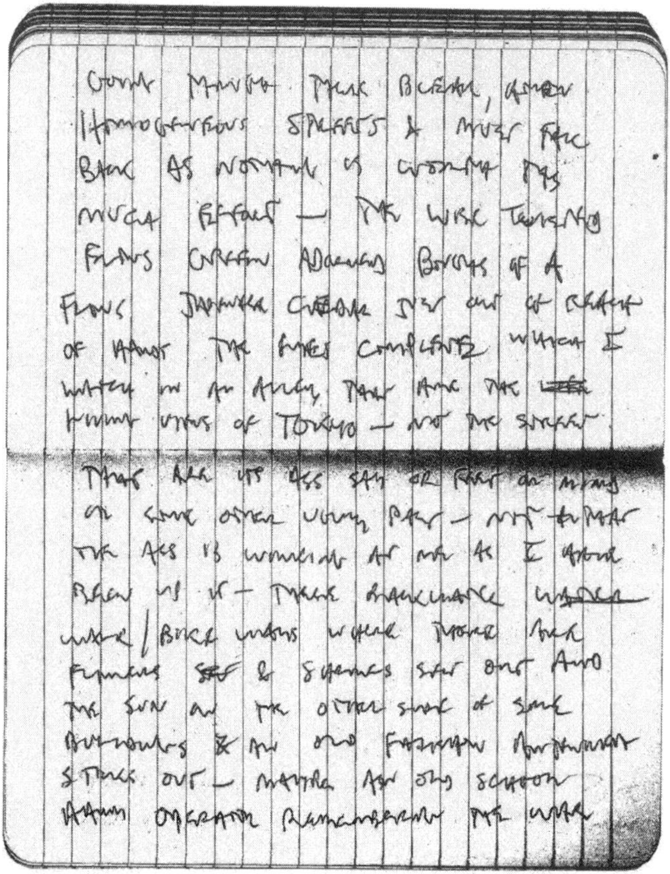
OF TOKYO — NOT THE STREET

putting a signal out into the
Cocteauan spheres receiving
signals from inner space
—

unlike Bernadette who doesn't
need one
—

that for me is aching feet & thirst
for a decent Kirin which I get
from Family Mart & sit in a niche
in the corner of a small office
building door at last at rest
though I need to piss,
which I may around the corner
when the neighborhood bar
opens,
my last conscious hours in
Tokyo
—

& then I've landed here after
veering off to pee in the park a
bright-lit bar w/ a kind hostess
whose brought me pickled
something & a Kirin out a soda
fountain tap & now I am sitting at
a low bar w/ a view of the
kitchen & writing smoking like I
used to do in New York & Paris
& a liberality of consciousness
—

a signal that is
—

comes over me that I have
arrived &

that I may never leave or as long
as my thirst for this & my money
may last
—
I need about 300 yen for a last
train tomorrow
—
& there is even a rectangular
mirror in front of me reflecting
one quarter of me or my chest
out the off-center portion of
which beats my heart if I could
find it,
I am so excited,
realizing I walked past this place
twice though it wasn't open & I
wasn't ready & now I am having
a second beer & think I can
afford four which would leave
me well ashore the land of bliss
if not blissto,
which is Japanese for Edo,
which was the planting of this
garden I had wanted to visit to
stand among old things & get
some perspective as everything
is watching her husband in a

white jacket & cap working the
kitchen the size of a closet
staked w/ walls of things & frig &
stove units to feed the
neighborhood army presses on
as he smiles & nods &
understands as the inhabitants
of this island,
as I have come to feel,
do
—

the lines as beginning to get
fuzzy
—

as they are Inexpressionist of
smoking & drinking in one place
in a real Japanese bar & wishing
I were twenty-three to really put
this scene to use beyond
acknowledgement of its
perfection from my western
decadent one in the last hours of
the fire escape,
& it no longer matters if I keep
going or not
—

barring missing flight out
—

& as I wrote have enough for
four Kirin's which must mean
something in Tarot
—

the four of cups
—

& we're laughing & the gaijin is

while [illegible] & cap working the kitchen the size of a closet stacked with vats of dishes & frogs & stock [illegible] to feed the [illegible] army press on as we swethere & moss & undergrowths as the [illegible] of this island as I have come to feel do the [illegible] of [illegible] to get fuzzy as they have [illegible] live of smoking & drinking in our [illegible] in a [illegible] Japanese bar & [illegible] I wer

23 to [illegible] for this [illegible] [illegible] acknowledgement of its [illegible] [illegible] my [illegible] [illegible] out on the last hours of the fire escape & it no [illegible] matters if I [illegible] going or not — [illegible] missing fucker out — & I was writing a hank [illegible] for four [illegible] watch must [illegible] [illegible] in Tarot terms — the four of cups — & we're [illegible] at the [illegible]'s

smiling & we're having a grand
time & I feel like Pierre re-acting
the dancing bear though its only
quarter to six in Sumida-cho
—
chucking more & more of myself
into the model
—
to hell w/ spacetime even if it is
our only sensation
—
the diamond at the end of light
—
& if they just dim it in this place
by half we'd be there
—
if there were more shadows to
trace across the arrows what
this is made of
—
namely mystery
—
dwelling as here coming through
"heaven" "reflection" &
"happiness" would get to "I am
happy,"
& she crossed her arms across
her chest & bowed as I did
enough for another beer to leave
room for noodle shop as,
thinking,
I return to this universe of one
thing after the next,
which I want to leave

SMILING & ... WE'RE HAVING A GRAND
TIME & I FEEL ... CON'T SISTER
RE-WATCHING THE DANCING BEAR TATTOO
ITS OWN QUALITY IT SAYS TO THE SUNWA-
CH CHROBIN MORE & MORE OF MYSELF
INTO THE (FIRE) — TO HAVE W/ SPACETIME
EVEN IF IT IS OUR ONLY SALVATION — THE
... AT THE END OF NIGHT — & IF
... JUST DIM THE LIGHT IN THIS PLACE
... WILL WE BE ... — IF THERE WHERE

MORE SISTERS ... ...
ALWAYS OF THIS PLACE THAT IS MADE OF
... NAMELY MYSTERY — AS THERE
... ... "HEAVEN" "PERFECTION" &
... ... GO TO "I AM HAPPY"
& SHE CROSSED ... HER ARMS ACROSS
HER CHEST AND BOWED AS I DID ENOUGH
FOR ANOTHER BEER TO HAVE ROOM FOR
ANY MOTHER SHIP AS THANKFUL I RETURN
TO THE UNIVERSE OF OUR TOWN AFTER
THE NEXT WATER I WANT TO LEAVE

like a medicant in a cave or a
man sitting w/ his dame,
in his command of the bar sitting
drinking & smoking & talking
instead of writing in a book
words words words that I see
could get pretty ugly pretty
quickly if they could see what a
degenerate I could be,
not writing conventional prose
yet rather one that rhymes w/
the end of time where we all
meet in the land of strange
scripts written in a language of
spirit,
as like the tail of a dragon who
remains close by waves over me
her scent that has the taste of
Diesel what w/ what she must
put up w/ what we all do living
on time borrowed from her,
in-part Cretaceous

—

not Edo

—

period powering

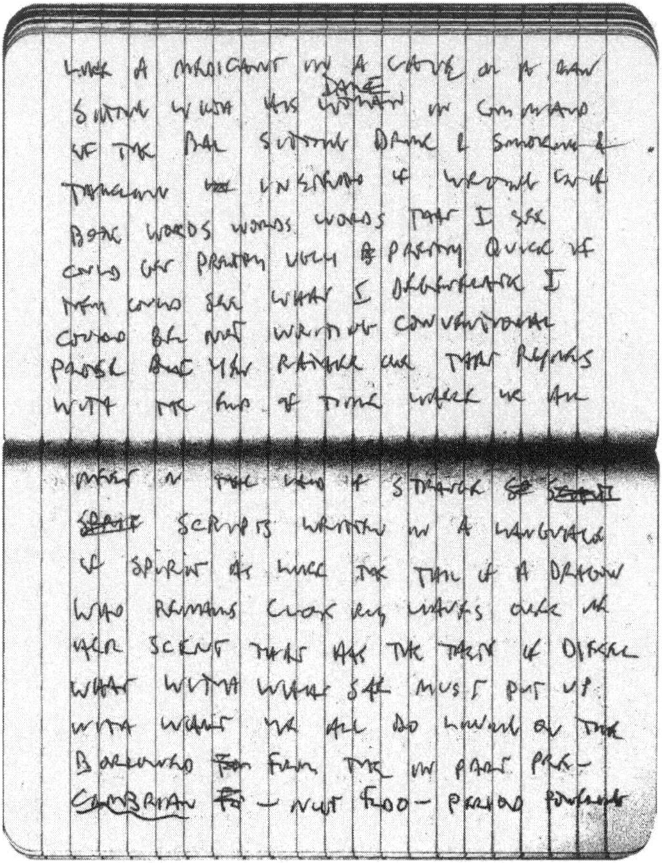

our chariots & not all of them of
the sun watching the news,
which I think as a compromise
Spicer won't approve,
the sound of a madhouse in the
gathering stillness in its marriage
w/ the tragic w/ only one or two
of its servants have I slept in this
slalom of human being,
the efficacy of which I have
sometimes doubted,
arriving right & left remaining in
the guise of a gaijin such as I am
a barbarian who hardly fits in the
toilet in the back in which you
squat if you want to take a dump
which would be a nice
reconciliation w/ Europe for
America to adopt,
though I doubt we could ever
make that fit or fitter

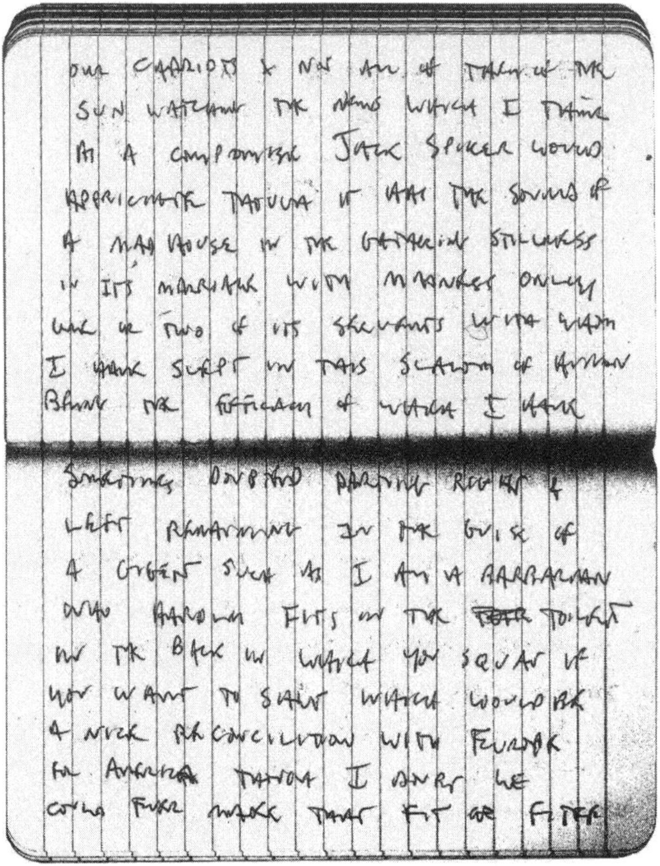
OUR CHARIOTS & NOW ALL OF TALK OF THE
SUN WATCHING THE NEWS WHICH I THINK
AS A COMPROMISE JACK SPICER WOULD
APPRECIATE THOUGH IT WAS THE SOUNDS OF
A MADHOUSE IN THE GATHERING STILLNESS
IN ITS MARRIAGE WITH MADNESS ONLY
ONE OR TWO OF ITS SERVANTS WITH WHOM
I HAVE SLEPT IN THIS SEASON OF HUMAN
BEING THE EFFICACY OF WHICH I HAVE
SOMETIMES DOUBTED PARTING RIGHT &
LEFT REMAINING IN THE GUISE OF
A GUEST SUCH AS I AM A BARBARIAN
WHO HARDLY FITS IN THE ~~FOR~~ TOILET
IN THE BACK IN WHICH YOU SQUAT IF
YOU WANT TO SHIT WHICH WOULD BE
A NICE RECONCILIATION WITH EUROPE
FOR AMERICA THOUGH I DOUBT WE
COULD EVER MAKE THAT FIT OR FITTER

such as a verse line locks life to
words lost in a pattern that won't
make you sick,
such as as on the precipice of
which I feel tighten through me
like a dragon unfurling a last
Kirin out of the taps,
& so like that flight a
convergence on the end of the
rhyme that through the fog of
beers I feel encroaching,
as does not time in sleep end?
    Tokyo never does I
understand,
though you'd have to work for it
—
as the line bumps up against
everything that has ever been or
may be radiating into dust,
or that for which it is a
euphemism,
which is us,
among whom I am the focus of a
lot of attention

SUCH AS A VERSE OF LOVE LOOKING
LIFE TO WORLDS WHERE WORLDS FOR A
A PATTERN THAT WON'T MAKE YOU
SOUL SUCH AS IN AS OF THE PRESENCE
OF WHICH I FEEL TIGHTEN THROUGH ME
LIKE A DRAGON UN FULFILLED A WAY
VICTORY ONE OF THE DAYS AND SO MUCH
THAT FURTHER A CONVERGENCE ON THE FIND OF
THE FUTURE THAT THROUGH THE FOG OF

RAGING I FEEL EVERYTHING AT WORK
NOT THE F IN SLEEP FIND 3 TOKYO
RATHER DOES I UNDERSTAND THROUGH WHO
WANT TO WORK FOR IT — AS THE LINE
OF BEING AGAINST EVERYTHING THAT HAS
EVER BEEN OR MAY BE RADIATING INTO
THE DUST OF THAT FROM WHICH IT IS
A EUPHORISM WHICH IS US OF WHOM
I AM THE FOCUS OF A LOT OF ATTENTION

127

at the corner of the bar sunk in
behind my heroic last beer
(
is this my fifth w/ the Family Mart
Kirin?
)
as my hostess plies w/ pleas to
eat yet I am holding out for my
noodle friend to whom I want to
press one of my books as
though they were real & might
stop it
—
what
—
the nightmare to which Joyce
likened history & longed to
escape or awake from it as they
may who are its inhabitants
bowing to nothing we cannot
name or blame as the waves
close behind us as they did in
Wakamasu-cho the alleys all
repaved & the walls all
rearranged & I have to say in the
toire there's a wall clock that
reads 6:35 & a wall calendar of
the

days of December presided over
by a sumo wrestler squatting in
the ring in traditional vestments
of knots of white & tawny loin
cloth a dragon on his back & a
Shinto priest & his arms
outstretched eyes glistening to
something off frame unseen just
like the mission I am on,
which has something to do w/
the dead such as she is not as
she makes her attractive course
glimmer,
river of wide open stretches,
or what does past human flaw
which the Japanese by any
measure
—

except verse
—

seek to avoid & so to find her
willing to rock her dark strong
waves before me promise of the
rising of the sun realm that at
this juncture is now pure con-

DAYS OF DECEMBER PERCHED OVER HIM A
SUMO WRESTLER SQUATTING IN THE RAW
IN TRADITIONAL DRESS OR OF KNOTS OF CLOTH
LOIN CLOTH WITH HIS ARMS OUTSTRETCHED
FINES GUSTOMENT T SOMETHING OFF FRANK
UNSEEN JUST LIKE THE MISSION I AM
ON, WHICH HAS SOMETHING TO DO WITH
THE DEAD SUCH AS SHE IS NOT AT HAND

MAKES HER ATTRACTIVE COARSH GENUINE
RIVER OF WHAT OPEN STRETCHES OR
WHAT USES PAST HUMAN FLAW WHERE THE
THINGS AND ANY MEASURE - RICKETY VERSE-
STRIC TO THE QUOD AND SO TO FIND HER
WILLING TO ROCK HER DARK STRAND
WAVES BEFORE HER PROMISE OF
HER RISING OF THE SUN REASON THAT
AT THIS TENEBRE IS NOW PURER CONT

gestural waving in the direction
of our lives,
versus just being here rolling
another dart dreaming from the
place the poem comes from,
Sumida-cho at a very primordial
noodle bar shop dreaming what
rends means & ends,
& Hermes more than anyone
else or what dares to be human
who has run out of money to
expend
—
thank god
—
on beer as I am really nearly
holding on writing into a more &
more finite space hours from my
flight & really enjoying my now-
self enacting a bear,
which sounds like beer w/ whom
I am now dancing stepping on
her toes made of effervescent
gold or

GESTURAL WAVING IN THE DIRECTION OF
ONE LIVES VERSUS JUST BEING KILLED
RIGHT AND ANOTHER DART DREAMING FOR
THE PLACE THE POEM COMES FROM SUNDAY-
CHO AT A VERY ~~BATING~~ ~~DETAIL~~
PRIMORDIAL NOODLE BAR SHOP DREAMING
WHAT WRENTS MEANS & FINDS &
AFFIRMS MORE THAN ANYONE ELSE OF
WHAT DARES TO BE HUMAN WHO HAS

RUN OUT OF MONEY TO RHYTHM OF
THANK GOD — ON BEER AT I AM ~~NOTHING~~
NEARLY WEARILY HEADING ON WEARING
INTO A MORE & MORE FINITE SPACE WHERE
FROM MY FUTURE AND READILY ENJOYING
MY NOW SELF SWALLOWING A ~~BEER~~ BEAR
WHERE SEEMS LIKE BEER WITH WHOM I
AM NOW DANCING SPREAD ON HER TOES
MUCH OF ~~EFFE~~ EFFERVESCENT GOLD AL

133

perhaps we can't take too long
in paradise & so were expelled,
as I must very soon be & absent
regret yet present supreme
gladness heave my way back to
Kuramae & my heart is breaking
—

& then I am in the subway
wondering where exactly I am
though knowing inordinately &
knowing I need to do a quick
search of my body to locate the
ticket I am paying or have & I'm
just happy to be imparting the
conviviality I feel to be among
such noble fellow human slaves
on cells,
each one their own,
yet the same as are all our
brains,
w/ a light layer of cultural
algorithms on the top of which
we identify,
& ride through infinitudes of
surprise,
which include if I will ever get out
alive
—

as I rise god knows where to this

PERHAPS WE SHALL. I FEEL TOO LONG IN
PARADISE & SO WILL PROBABLY AS I MUST
VERY SOON BE & ABSENT REGRET MY
PRESENT SUPREME GLADNESS THANK MY
WAY BACK TO KURAMAE AND MY HEART
IS BREAKING — & THEN I AM IN THE
SEVENTH HEAVEN WHERE BECAUSE I AM
THORNE KURAMAE IN OPPORTUNITY & ENOUGH
I USED TO BE A GOOD STRANGER OF MY BODY
TO LEAVE THE THREE & THE PART OF

WHERE I STILL SAY WHAT TO BE WONDERING
THE CONVERSATION I FEEL TO BE AMONG
SUCH NOBLE FELLOW HUMAN SLAVES N
CAN KNOW OF THEIR OWN LIFE THE
SAME AS ARE OUR BRAINS WHEN A
LIVING LIGHT OF CULTURE ALGO RHYTHM)
AN THE TOP AT WHICH WE RISE
PREVIOUS REFOR LATEST REMEMBER 4 OF
SUNRISE WHICH INCLUDE IF I HAVE
EVER GOT OUT ALIVE — AS I RISE
GOD KNOWS WHERE TO THE THAT

deep Earth blow of winds rising
around climbing this fantastic in-
city obstacle of a flight of 108
steps which you must take to get
here gazing into the voluminous
world of human explosions,
each going off in different
directions that all meet in one
which is not for long on beloved
blue planet,
an eye of which is Tokyo w/ its
crooked walk enclosed in a
perfect order that can only
express itself in decadence as
we wish all civilization will too
break apart into
—
& it does now as we breathe like
the surface of

a Tokyo subway car folks
craning into their cells mostly or
in immediate view everybody & I
mean everybody is,
which in the 12-year span since
its introduction is ineffable & in
fact there's an air of social
acceptance around it
—

like the mask is obligatory action
wear the cell its equivalent
leisure one
—

clawing w/ eyes & ears & fingers
the walls of the cave we are
whistling through so far
underground we can't even see
it
—

the layer
—

& I made the noodle shop &
there was this moment
balancing between my friend
having come in w/ the book & it
was closing turned the rules a

little aside & drinking an Ishi
talking in broken language
realized touching myself I was
light this vessel through which I
am talking to you about how I
thought I lost it,
& had the experience
—
because of having lost & had
then found so many things over
the last few days' vista
—
of a crow touching the back of
my neck,
& realize I am back along the
Sumida as a woman on my right
seeing my agitation

& standing bowing out to retrace
steps,
though at the same time
immediately accepting the loss
of this ossification in the
balances that have
—
even let alone I have been
—
lost,
& immeasurably accept its loss
though w/ the knowing Japanese
society would recognize the
imbalance having dutifully
inscribed the start of this life w/
an email
—
samtruitt@gmail.com
—
I was assured actually of its
return amen,
which is how society ought to
have been w/ each of us looking
out for the next one until the next
be-

A statement brought out to
portray ones presence at the
same time unconditionally ac-
cepting the loss of this ossuary
in the knowledge that I have never
let know I have before lost
accepted its loss though with the
knowing that another society would

would reconsider the imbalance
having ounfrom inscribed the
start of this like with the guard
I was assured actuality of us
return anew which is how
societys ought to have been with
each of us looking out for
the next until the next but

side the Sumida gently rolling
me rocking inexorably from deep
within what is
—

as she turned & not bowing
handed me this the surface of
which I kiss w/ words like the
waves that flutter beyond the
grave the stones of which in
Yamato are amazing
—

& again reference to the Shinto,
how while Xristianity may
provide color & Buddhism calm,
it rules the land of the dead &
proves an awesome use of real
estate
—

& even visiting the goddess of
beauty on the stalked dead
lovely lake of Ueno in which she
is situated,
though it might be a he & might
as well be omnidirectionally,
as I look on the site of its
construction
—

having dug a further niche in the
cliffs of Kuramae in which to
pitch its mesh-encased

walls & load & pits & chain-link
fence & there is nothing that
looks more desolate as a site in
which there is active creature
such as I see a near half block
of at least 20 soaring stories into
the sky along the river w/ a
setback at its 9 or 10th floor,
a jumbo principally residential
yet who knows w/ a retail
component at the ground level
—
where I am in infinite gratitude
for where I am though cold &
hungry,
as the perfect society is
lightweight & mobile like Tokyo
yet also like these travelers w/
whom I have fallen

WALLS & CAVITIES & CARRION LIKE FLESH
& THERE IS NOTHING THAT LOOKS ANY MORE
DISGUSTING AS IN A SITE IN WHICH
THERE IS ACTIVE CREATURE SUCH AS
I SAW A NEAR HALF-BLOCK OF AT
LEAST 20-8 SQUARE FLOORS AND FOR SURE
WITH A SET RATE OF 65 FT A 10TH FLOOR
A JUMBO PRINCIPALLY RESIDENTIAL YET

WHO KNOWS FOR A RETAIL CONVENTION AS
THE GROUND LEVEL WHERE I AM IN
INFINITE GRATITUDE FOR WHICH I AM
THOUGH COLD & HUNGRY AS THE PRESENT
SITUATION IS LIKELY WITHOUT ANY MOMENT
LIKE SAVING MY ABSOLUTE ~~PEACE OF MIND~~
PRINCIPLES UNTIL WHOM I HAVE FORWARD

in as I bite there into some 7-11
hot meat skewer things I can
hear hearsay "I don't want to
die,"
which is actually what the PA is
playing,
& yet why not drop into the water
of her as I eat more meat & drink
more beer as a barbarian ought,
& I walk no more miles sitting at
my station as I hear a song
about Californication across the
Pacific where I once lived & has
grated these last hours before
being shot out a hole no sky can
hold & realize soon I will have to
let go this hook on which I've
hung this rung of experience off
which more

visible & invisible are hung &
each the weight of light & mobile
& tingling,
as the wind rises & the music
too though more schlock
estadus unites stuff that makes
one want to roop,
which you wonder I might after
all the crap I've ingested & Kirin I
fear catch up w/ moi & words if
they were an ocean would
desert me as though that
mattered,
or cloud or drop in & out the sea
of quiddity trying as we pass to
be as friendly as possible to
everything visible & invisible as
the light that speaks things when
you relax

VISIBLE & INVISIBLE ARE HUGE & FACT
IR LIGHT WEIGHT & MASSIVE & THOUGHT
AS THE WIND RISES & THE MUSIC TOO
THROUGH MORE SLOWLY BETWEEN UNLESS
STILL THAT MAKES ONE WANT TO RUSH
WHICH YOU WONDER WHETHER IS MOTION
AFTER ALL THE SLOW CRAP I'VE
HEARD & KNOW I HAVE MAY

WORDS CATCH UP WITH ME & WORDS
IF THEY WERE AN OCEAN WOULD DISRUPT
ME AS THOUGH THEY MATTERS A COULD
ALROSE IN & OUT THE SKY OF QUANTITY
THINK IF WE PASS TO ME AT EVERYTHING
IS POSSIBLE TO EVERYTHING VISIBLE AND
INVISIBLE AS THE LIGHT THAT
SPARKLE DANCES WHEN YOU RELAX

them trying to pull out the hook
the fat bald old man put in place
of a face it could gaze out the
maze that when you face things
we are in,
& the decision is either fight it or
explore the flow & each of us
become its revolution,
which is the heart of it in Tokyo
as everything seems a trope to
be what takes off clothes &
swims out into this river in a cool
breeze in want of nothing in
perfect equilibrium the man

THEY DRINK TO PULL DOWN THE HOOK
THE FAT BALD OLD MAN PUT IN PLACE
OF A FAITH IT COULD GATHER OUT
OF THE MAZE THAT WHEN YOU
FACE THINGS WE ARE IN A
OUR DECISION IS BIGGER THAN IT OR
FREEDOM THE FROM & WANT OF US

BEFORE A REVOLUTION WAKE IS
THE HEART OF IT IN TOKYO AS
EVERYTHING SEEKS A TRIPLE TO AR TO
WEAR TAKES OFF CLOTHES & SWIMS
OUT INTO THIS RIVER IN A COOL
BREEZE IN WANT OF NOTHING IF IN
PERFECT EQUILIBRIUM THE MAN

of sorrows wears to the
crowning of leaving now Japan
rambling on in words when I
cannot present to you the gate
to its subterranean primordial
consciousness,
as I discover Prague is super
liberal & Donna Summer plays
like the last books of Olson of I
will survive over & over again
—
as I gaze on this floor this page I
stand on dancing on the head of
a pen what happens to people
while this is playing inside
outside them
—
as a soft wind blows over the
invisible man hung w/ no fears
past what words heal & I'm

BEGINNING TO FEEL THE STRAIN LISTENING
TO VOICES & THEIR ANSWER & A
MAN WITH VIOLENT COUGHS & OUR AIR
EXPLOSIVES IN THE HANDS OF BEINGS
WE MAY OR MAY NOT SEE CROW
INTO CONSCIOUS HUMAN BEINGS
WHO KNOWS AS THREATS BEEN LESS
THAN THE DREAM OF A UNIVERSE

HANG ON THAN A LANTERN
ACROSS A DIM FIELD ON GREEN
ITS WALLS OF WOOD DOES
DESCRIBING SOME GOD THE
WATER HANGS OFF WHAT IS FOR
                   AS SUN RISES
OUT OF AIR THE SUN THIS BOOK WINDS
POUR OVER

beginning to feel its strain
listening to voices & their
absences,
& a man w/ violence coughs &
our age explosives in the
hands of babies we may or
may not see grow into
conscious human beings,
who knows,
as there's been less than the
dream of a universe hung on
than what a lantern across a
dim field on green its walls of
wood does
—
describing some god the water
hangs off what/how she rises
out of air the sun this book
words pour over
—


23.Nov—03.Dec.2019

bala!

Sam Truitt was born in Washington, DC, and raised there and in Tokyo, Japan. He is the author of the ten works in the Vertical Elegies series, among others in print and other media, and the co-editor of *In|Filtration: An Anthology of Innovative Poetry from the Hudson River Valley* and *Eating the Colors of a Lineup of Words: The Early Books of Bernadette Mayer*. Robert Creeley likened Truitt to "a contemporary Everyman," and he is the recipient, among other recognitions, of numerous Fund for Poetry awards, a Contemporary Poetry Award from the University of Georgia, and a Howard Fellowship. The producer and a co-host of the podcast Baffling Combustions and Director of Station Hill Press, he lives in Woodstock, NY. For more, visit: samtruitt.org